MW00901075

A Kindred Spirit

Maxine Cardinal Wehry
USMCWR 1943-1945

To: Jean!
Semper Fi.! Enjoy!
Maxine Cardinal Wehry
4 MA Convention
Philadelphia, PA
Aug. 31 - Sept. 4, 2012

Copyright © 2011 by Maxine Cardinal Wehry
Cover photograph by Cpl. Parker
Women Marines Association and Women in Military Service of
America logos used with permission
All rights reserved.
No part of this book may be reproduced in any form or by any
electronic or mechanical means including information storage and
retrieval systems, without permission in writing from the author.
The only exception is by a reviewer, who may quote short excerpts
in a review.

A Kindred Spirit

A Memoir by:
Maxine Cardinal Wehry
USMCWR - 1943-1945

Kindred: A body of persons related or of similar nature or character.

Spirit: A dominant tendency or feeling, a vigorous sense of membership.

Acknowledgements

My heartfelt thanks to the following for their help, interest and encouragement. Without you, there would be no story to write nor book to read.

First, there is my father Anthony L. Cardinal (now deceased) who signed my consent form allowing me to join the United States Marine Corps Women's Reserve at age twenty.

PFC Lonnie Crowell, USMC, IN
PFC Gene Marshall, USMC, NC
PFC Leonard J. Mooney, USMC, NJ
Jeanne Wehry Rittinger, GRI
Susan M. Wehry, MD
Joseph P. Wehry, USMCR
Bonnie Hosse
Pam Hinds-Pajac and husband, Joe Pajac, USMC
Richard Rogers, Sr. and wife, Susan
Herschell Hamm, USMC
Robert Reuter, USMC
Donald E. Roudebush, USMC (Ret)
Col. David Severance, USMC (Ret)
Heaven Cacamese
Gulfport Writer's Workshop Group
Women Marines Association
Women in Military Service of America

Preface

A kindred spirit, an esprit-de-corps, exists in the hearts of Marines and is epitomized in their motto, "Semper Fidelis, Always Faithful." It's the encouragement I needed to write my story.

During WWII, I was a young Woman Marine stationed at the Marine Corps Air Station, Ewa, Oahu, Territory of Hawaii. On the weekend of May 26-27, 1945, I met a young Marine survivor of Iwo Jima. He was with the Fifth Marine Division and Easy Company, who had raised our flag, "Old Glory," on Mt. Suribachi.

We were Marines and Hoosiers, thousands of miles from our homes in Evansville and Vincennes, Indiana. Being only sixty miles apart, we shared a history of rivalry in school sports. A kindred spirit of home existed. When we parted, PFC Lonnie Crowell gave me a Japanese "Rising Sun" flag as a souvenir.

Fifty-four years later, I discovered on the flag, three fading signatures: Lonnie Crowell, IND; Gene Marshall, NC; and Leonard J. Mooney, NJ.

In 2007 I started a journey to find the three people to connect with the three names. Come share my adventure.

Lonnie Crowell, Maxine Cardinal and unidentified Marine

Maxine Wehry and Leonard J. Mooney with flag

Chapter One

It was July 6, 2010, and I was on my way from Gulfport, Florida, to Tampa International Airport; destination: Burlington, Vermont, with a stopover in New Jersey. Brenda, my daughter Jeanne's friend, was chauffeuring me on the first leg of my journey. Crossing the Howard Franklin Causeway, we nervously watched the dark clouds hovering over the water.

"Sure hope those clouds dissipate and don't head northeast," I quipped.

"Me too," Brenda replied. "I hope I get back home before it starts raining. It looks as if a good downpour will be happening soon."

"Just drop me off at Delta. I can handle the rest. You hurry home."

Checking in, I reminded the man at the counter I had ordered a wheelchair. Since turning eighty I had discovered it's much easier and smarter to use this convenience to arrive at the boarding zone without being short of breath, tired, and hoping my heart murmur didn't murmur too loudly.

A friendly gentleman soon arrived to be my escort. I recognized him, and as he pushed my chair I thanked him again for having been so helpful to me the previous year. I asked about the weather and he was a little hesitant answering me.

"There is a storm headed this way, but it's moving fast. It should be through here by the time you leave."

He placed my chair near the large windows, where I could gaze out at the tarmac and watch the planes arriving and leaving. My plane wasn't leaving for two hours, and this would help pass the time.

The storm came in quickly and darkness enveloped the area. Rain cascaded down the window panes, forming a curtain and obliterating our view.

A hush descended over the crowd, especially those waiting to board the plane outside the window. Now we saw only a silhouette as the brilliant flashes of lightning illuminated the darkness outside. When the storm became less threatening, the passengers began boarding their planes and were soon on their way.

Flying has never been an enjoyment for me, and as I waited for my plane to arrive, I became more nervous. The sky still looked ominous and the rumbling of the thunder and the flashes of lightning still dancing in the sky was unnerving as we boarded. However, I convinced myself that nothing was going to dampen my enthusiasm.

The plane took off and began bouncing and wobbling as we entered the dark clouds. Sitting by the window, I watched the lightning still zigzagging across the heavens, and held onto the arm rests with white-knuckled fingers and prayed, "Please God, don't let the lightning strike our plane!"

We cheered as sunlight and white puffy clouds appeared. I relaxed as the reason for my exhilaration flashed across my mind.

My daughter Susan had invited me for a visit. When I realized I could fly into Newark, New Jersey and make connections to Burlington, I became aware we could meet Leonard J. Mooney in Hackettstown, New Jersey. I had learned he was the sole survivor of the three Marines whose names were on my souvenir Japanese 'Rising Sun' flag given to me sixty-five years ago. He was now a very important part of a book I was attempting to write. With the help of his nephew Richard "Dick" Rogers, Sr., our plans were made.

Chapter Two

Sixty-five years! How time had flown! I closed my eyes and began to explore the events which had transpired in my life that now were sending me on this incredible journey.

It seemed such a short time ago that I had graduated from Lincoln High School in Vincennes, Indiana. The year was nineteen forty-one, and I was living in Indianapolis, having accepted a scholarship to the International Beauty School of Cosmetology.

The sneak attack by the Japanese on Pearl Harbor December 7 had almost annihilated our Naval Armada. Nearby, the Army, Navy and Marine Corps Air Forces had suffered the same destruction. Human causalities were astronomical. December 8, 1941, we declared war on Japan, and three days later, Germany and Italy, Allies of Japan, declared war on the United States. When we retaliated, World War II enveloped the world. With patriotic fervor, men, women, and boys rushed to enlist in the armed services to serve their country.

I was eighteen. Since twenty was the acceptable age for women to enlist if a parent consented, I watched with interest as each armed service displayed their uniforms for women. None piqued my interest until February 13, 1943, when the United States Marine Corps Women's Reserve was established. Their uniform, especially the hat, was awesome!

"I'm going to be a Marine," I declared to anyone who would listen, but mainly to my boss, Paul Morelock.

First, I called my dad to ask if he'd sign my consent form when I'd turn twenty, October 7 of that year. He said yes! My mother had died when I was two years of age, and I often wondered if she would have been as eager to give her consent. I just knew I would look good in that hat! Green in color, with an accent of red cord above the peak; it went so well with the same green uniform, the khaki shirt and tie. A dark brown purse, matching gloves, and oxfords completed "the look." So military, so feminine, so smart. I would wear it proudly and serve my country.

October 7 arrived and my father signed my consent form.

A patron whose name I can't remember, and whose husband worked for the railroad, obtained two passes, and we traveled to Cincinnati, Ohio, where I could enlist.

Having failed to bring an important health report of a benign breast tumor, I was sent home, very disappointed. They also advised me to eat spaghetti and bananas to gain some weight, as I weighed below the required one hundred and ten pounds.

The following week, I sent in the report. A few days later they informed me to return November 15 to be sworn in to the Marine Corps. We traveled again to Cincinnati, where I was sworn in at one hundred eight pounds.

Pvt. Mildred Maxine Cardinal, USMCWR, 766861, returned to Indianapolis; and would serve her country for the duration of the war. The happiest and proudest person on that train was me!

I continued working at Paul's Barber and Beauty Shop on Michigan Avenue until the holiday rush was over. Then I left after a tearful good-bye to the Morelocks; to Charlene, my coworker; to Charlotte, my roommate; and to all my customers and friends. Christmas holidays were spent at home, where I awaited my orders for boot camp. They arrived the first week of January 1944. I was to be in Camp Lejeune, North Carolina, on January 24. The afternoon of January 22, I boarded the train for Washington, DC. We arrived the following morning and I met several other Women Marines in civilian clothes. We toured the Capitol and the two houses of Congress, where I sat and wondered how anything could be accomplished in this chaotic place. Absolute confusion! Is today any different? Touring the various monuments was thrilling, especially the Lincoln Memorial. He had always been my favorite president, and I stood in awe before his statue.

At 1830 Marine time, we all met at Union Station and boarded the train for Camp Lejeune to begin our six weeks of basic training. I was assigned to Company B, Platoon 2 (which we later affectionately called the Goon Platoon), 25th Battalion, and Barracks 108. Sgt. Calhoun and Cpl. Benda were our leaders, who soon transformed us into a group of sharp Women Marines.

We were taught how to make a neat, tight bed with squared corners. Every article in our foot and clothes lockers had its place, and it better be in its place, neatly hung and properly folded. Our shoes had to be polished, uniforms clean and pressed, hair short and off the collar of our uniforms. Oh yes, the seams in our lisle (cotton) hose had to be straight! Light make-up was permitted, we had our own colors of lipstick and nail polish. As I remember, both were from Revlon, in the colors of Scarlet Slipper, Rosy Future, Bravo, and Montezuma Red.

We were up every morning to eat, march, exercise, and attend classes to learn about our government and the Corps. It made for a very busy day. Aptitude tests were taken to measure our IQ. I deliberately flunked my typing test so I wouldn't have to work in an office. I wanted to be a mechanic and "Free A Marine To Fight," just as they had advertised. While precision marching, our drill instructor, Sgt. Troy M. Dasher, gave me a small piece of wood to hold in my right hand so I wouldn't confuse my right and left commands. We had gas mask drills, which were scary. Our immunization tests turned into a quarantine of my barracks. I was allergic to one of the shots and they thought I had measles! Eventually the girls forgave me.

Virginia "Ezzie" Evans and I led the singing to and from chow and anywhere else we were permitted to do so. Pulling pranks on one another by short-sheeting beds led to a lot of laughter in the evenings. I still cringe when I think about the trick we played on Ilene Mohler. A raw egg was placed in her bed and cracked. Then we had a surprise inspection and had to work hard to get her bed perfect. Had we been caught, we would have been severely punished, maybe even discharged. (At Easter that year, and in my new assignment, I came home to the barracks and found a decorated egg in the middle of my bed – I knew Mohler had arrived!)

Near the time of graduation, we presented a large musical stage show. My job was hair and make-up. On the night of graduation, we had a dance. That was my first and only rendezvous with male Marines at Camp Lejeune. A young handsome Marine from Connecticut gave me his salty Marine emblem for my hat. It became a prized possession. Unfortunately, while stationed at El Toro, my hat and emblem were stolen and, I feel almost certain, were given to a civilian girl. (I know the Marines who did it, their demeanor later gave them away.)

Our graduation, as I recall, was March 7, 1944. My new assignment read: Beauty Operator, Marine Corps Air Station, El Toro, California.

So much for "Freeing A Marine To Fight!"

My Inspiration

Maxine Cardinal and father, Anthony L. Cardinal

Maxine Cardinal, 19, in front of Paul's Barber & Beauty Shop

Roommate Charlotte Langoff and
Maxine Cardinal

Paul and Bonnie Morelock

Lts. Casteel, Paulding, DeSpain, and Green

Company B, Platoon 2, Camp Lejeune, Jan 1944

Dottie Egolf, Camp Lejeune

Platoon Leaders, Cpl. Benda and Sgt. Calhoun

Maxine Cardinal, USMCWR

Chapter Three

Our journey to California was via the southern route on a very long and slow-moving troop train. Cars were hooked and unhooked along the way, and at times it seemed we sat for hours on side tracks. The trip took us four or five days. I remember the food was good, and I was introduced to grits, a favorite I still enjoy, especially at breakfast.

Several of the girls, including my best friend and bunky, Dottie Egolf from Ohio, departed somewhere along the way for Norman, Oklahoma, and Mechanics School. Without me!

"Mind if I share this seat?"

I looked up and saw the girl several of us had envied at graduation. She was one of the few who had received a uniform purse. She had acted as if the rest of us were peons and she was Miss High-and-mighty. I had taken an immediate dislike to her.

"Its empty," I replied, with little enthusiasm. "My bunky just left for Norman, Oklahoma."

She sat down and introduced herself. "I'm Jean Lowenthal, but everyone calls me Corky."

"I'm Maxine Cardinal, and you can call me anything you wish. My friends call me Max."

We sat in silence for awhile.

"Where are you from Corky?"

"Philadelphia, Pennsylvania. You?"

"Vincennes, Indiana."

Silence. You might as well clear the air, I thought.

"At graduation, why were you such a smart aleck regarding your purse? You knew we all felt bad because ours hadn't arrived from the manufacturer."

"Oh, that? I was mostly joking. My cousin had joined earlier and didn't like it, so was discharged. She gave me her purse as a parting gift. Didn't realize I'd made enemies."

"Well, you did."

It's hard to believe this meeting evolved into an enjoyable trip and a lifelong, beautiful friendship, but it did. Eventually, I was her maid of honor when she and Cy were married. Corky died in 1986.

We arrived in Los Angeles during an unprecedented torrential downpour. As we boarded our El Toro bus, I asked the driver, "Do you have pontoon boats available to get us into our barracks?" Everyone chuckled. To my surprise, my remark appeared in the base newspaper the following week.

Corky and I chose one of the double-decker bunks in a six-person cubicle. We had no argument who would sleep up top. I wanted it and she didn't.

We were soon joined by four other Women Marines from various parts of the United States: Imogene Bielack, from Michigan (I think); Mae Brady, New Jersey; her friend Pauline Jones, Ohio; and Elizabeth O'Hill from Oregon or Washington, who became Imogene's bunkmate. Elizabeth was the most shy of all and did very little socializing with us. It was a congenial group, however, and my nine months with them were great.

Maxine Cardinal and Jean "Corky" Lowenthal

Imogene Bielack

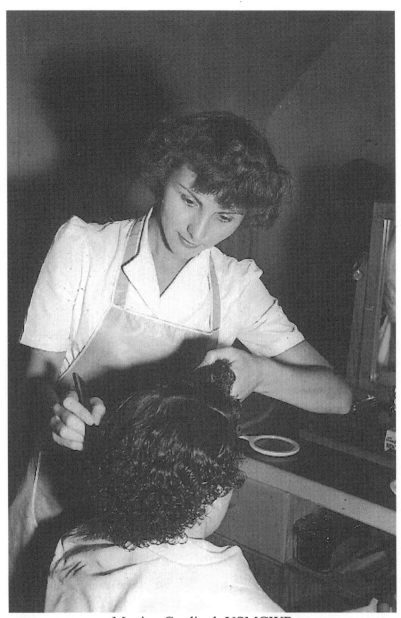

Maxine Cardinal, USMCWR
Beauty Shop, MCAS Oahu, Territory of Hawaii

Chapter Four

Dressed in my white work uniform, I went to the Beauty Shop, located at the end of the Post Exchange (PX) building. There were two other beauticians: 'Stormy' Lamb, a Lucille Ball redhead from Ohio, and Doris Lawson, a blonde from Corbin, Kentucky. I was the brunette in the trio. They were both so worldly, and I, who thought she knew it all, knew nothing. What a learning experience!

El Toro, my home for nine months, gave me some of my favorite lifetime memories.

"Anyone want to see Bing Crosby?" a voice yelled through the open door of the Beauty Shop. "He's in the PX with his brother Bob, Dan Topping, Sonja Heine's husband, and a group of officers." Having no customers, out the door I ran. After buying a chocolate milkshake, I sat down with several other awestruck girls. Looking at those beautiful dreamy blue eyes only two tables away, I picked up my shake, and the next thing I knew, my face and uniform were swathed in chocolate ice cream! What an embarrassment!

I still recall these words from an advertisement of Earl Carroll's Restaurant in Los Angeles: "Through These Portals Pass The Most Beautiful Girls In The World!" That's just how Pauline Jones, Mae Brady, Corky and I felt as we entered to celebrate my twenty-first birthday, October 7, 1944. It was a fun-filled Saturday night for four slightly inebriated Women Marines, who returned to the base on Sunday with headaches.

Now, I was old enough to have a beer with my friend Corky and our sailor friends John Thomas and 'Rosey.' We had met them in the Chicago train station as we returned from our furloughs. We had gotten on the same car as them and their friends, all from LST 240. They were a great bunch to travel with, as they entertained us with guitars, harmonicas, and an accordion. We sang, played cards, then slept, and the next days we did the same thing, until we arrived in Los Angeles.

The four of us dated on weekends, mostly at Corky's relatives,

Uncle Howard's home and the Fieldings in Long Beach. The week before I was twenty-one, we had gone to an obscure bar on the outskirts of Long Beach where the boys knew they could get a beer. It was against the law to serve alcohol to a table if any occupant was under twenty-one. They all ordered beer, and me, a 7-Up. I accidentally knocked Corky's beer off the table and into her purse, sitting on the floor. This turned into a catastrophe.

Arriving back at the base, we scrubbed, rinsed, and dried the articles in the purse, and double scrubbed the purse itself. We placed the purse on the windowsill to dry, and the contents were put in her locker, near our beds. We were awakened in the morning by Jonesy's screams. There were ants all over the windowsill, inside the purse, and across the floor to the locker. It was a chore finding something with which to spray our area, but two days later, we had fresh air and no ants!

As I returned from work one evening, I met Bielack entering the barracks after her late shift in Transportation. "Are you on duty Tuesday morning?" I asked. "I need a ride into Santa Ana to pick up supplies for the Beauty Shop. Lt. Ordeman said she would call and set up the time. It would be more fun if you could drive me there."

"I'm sure I can get that detail," she replied.

Monday evening, Bielack informed me we would be leaving at ten A.M., and she would also be taking a Marine officer to the Army Air Force base nearby. The next morning, the two of us found the officer waiting in front of the Administration Building, and we headed toward Santa Ana. He introduced himself, and we had an interesting and delightful conversation as we traveled. At the Air Force base, he joked with a group of Cadets who came over and talked with us as we waited for his return. I accomplished my mission, and as we traveled back to El Toro, we continued our three-way congenial conversation.

Recounting my meeting with this pleasant, unassuming officer to some friends, I learned he was our Legal Officer. He had the distinction of never losing a case involving enlisted personnel. The only case he had lost involved an officer.

Years later, imagine my surprise when I turned on the

television and saw this Marine officer, Senator Joseph McCarthy, being humiliated for his investigation of alleged card-carrying Communists. This brought an end to his political career. Did I hear or read later, when the files were declassified, they proved he had been right? Maybe I should check on that. Surely there is something on those websites I keep hearing about. Technology?

Well, I've always believed he was sincere in trying to protect our country. Call it esprit-de-corps or whatever, but to you, Senator Joseph McCarthy, Semper Fi Marine!

I loved El Toro and all my friends, but I was also adventuresome. During my school days, I had entertained myself for hours with the Book of Knowledge and dreamed of visiting or living in other places. So, when the Women Marines were permitted to serve in the Hawaiian Islands, I immediately signed to go, and was accepted.

The first phase of training was in San Diego, perhaps Camp Pendleton, I'm not sure. We were only there for a short time and spent our days in classes, hearing about how close we would be to the war zone, watching STD movies, and being told how the Islands affected our libido. The latter had been suggested by our future commanding officer, Major Crean. Calisthenics and swimming were a part of our exercise program. I have a fear of deep water and was not a swimmer, so the most frightening experience was jumping from a twenty foot or more diving board with a full pack! We placed one hand between our legs to protect the crotch. The other hand held the backpack and life jacket straps under our chin so we wouldn't break our necks. I've often wondered if this would have worked had we needed to abandon ship.

Thank God we only had to do that once in training! The girl in front of me froze with fear, and while I waited those agonizing minutes before her eventual jump, I made up my mind that I would just step off into space and let the Captain below save me!

One day they let us go out on the firing range. I don't remember what we were permitted to fire, but I have a couple targets in my scrapbook. They said I made marksman, but I never received a medal. Were those really mine?

From San Diego, we went to San Francisco, where the beauty operators attended Helene Curtis School of Cosmetology and were taught how to give the new machineless permanent waves, referred to as "Cold Waves," similar to those of today.

(Unfortunately, six months later, I became nauseous, couldn't stand the sight of food and lost ten pounds. From the tests, the doctors diagnosed that the chemical solutions were causing the reaction and the resulting malnutrition was treated with a nutrient-rich diet. Vitamin B and fortified milk shakes became my best friends!)

I was in the second, and most fortunate, of the overseas groups, as we traveled in style aboard the luxury cruise liner SS Lurline to Honolulu. Most of the girls traveled on various types of naval vessels, and under very bad conditions.

Our meals were served in a dining room with round tables covered with tablecloths. The waiter serving my table had stayed on board when the liner was commissioned into service by the government for troop deployments. He was a true clone of Jimmy Durante, nose and all. He was so funny and helpful. He advised those of us who were a little queasy to eat the crackers and drink the sodas he provided, and to stay topside in the fresh air and sit with our backs against the bulkhead. It worked for me. The second day I was fine.

Several of the girls stayed in their bunks, in the crowded, stale air of the staterooms, too ill to enjoy their trip. They missed our Aloha Dinner of filet mignon!

We arrived in Honolulu on February 25, 1945, five days after leaving San Francisco. My address was MCAS-61-AWRS-14, Ewa, Oahu, T. of H.

Our names and hometowns had been published in most surrounding camp newspapers, so our first few days were spent reconnecting with old friends, neighbors, and relatives. A sailor by the name of Klein from my hometown visited with me. He was leaving the next day and asked if he could call my folks to let them know I had arrived safely. I really appreciated that.

He also informed me another sailor, Harry Steininger, was stationed nearby. Harry was my neighbor and his sister Mary

Jane and I were great friends. We had accepted scholarships to the beauty school in Indianapolis after our graduation from high school and had roomed together. He gave me Harry's phone number, so we visited by phone, but never in person, as he was soon deployed elsewhere.

Shortly after the Beauty Shop opened in April, I looked up to see this giant of a man stooping to enter the door. Another Vincennes man had seen my name. He was Marion Youngstafel. (Years later, we had an unexpected reunion when we met while he was Sheriff and was directing traffic at an accident near my parents' home.)

There were three barracks in our complex, and I was assigned to Number 2, aptly called, as it was situated between one and three. It was so interesting working the front desk for a few nights when I first arrived. I enjoyed meeting the male Marines as they came to visit, or as one girl sarcastically remarked, "They just come to pick out their next conquest." In between interruptions, I'd play tic-tac-toe with some of them, and one presented me with a caricature of myself that he had drawn. It's in my scrapbook, so not all of them were looking for conquests. Some just wanted a friend.

My first day at the beach, I didn't heed the warnings of my friends about the sun's dangerous rays. Instead, Miss Know-it-all wore a two-piece bathing suit—very modest, nothing like the bikinis of today. The next day, I awoke very sick, burnt inside and out, from front to back! I couldn't seek medical aid, because it would mean forfeiture of pay and perhaps loss of my one stripe because of my stupidity. I suffered through it and continued mess hall duty, hiding it under a long-sleeved khaki shirt and long khaki trousers. It was torture! At night, my friends poured vinegar over my body and then saturated me with lotion or baby oil. My skin cracked and peeled for a month, but I had learned a very important lesson.

The first week on KP, I had a run-in with one of the cooks, Sgt. Cooley, another Hoosier, who reminded me of my oldest brother, Woodie. He reprimanded me for scraping off layers of burned-on grease he was letting accumulate so the food wouldn't stick. The pans looked a mess, and I had wanted to make a good impression.

I still remember the terrible odor permeating from those pans when used to cook cheap mutton chops. I had thrown mine in the garbage at lunchtime, thinking they were rotten pork chops!

I was put in charge of the Beauty Shop, no doubt a political gesture. Lt. Maude Paulding, my boss, was a good friend of Lt. Evelyn DeSpain, a customer of mine at El Toro. She and I had a bond between us. Her mother, like me, was from Indiana, and she had asked Lt. Paulding to look out for me. Maude and I remained friends until her death, November 15, 1985.

One day Lt. Paulding came into the shop and announced that I had to be promoted to Corporal. I pleaded with her not to change my status. As a PFC, I received overseas pay, plus extra PX pay, and as long as I remained below Corporal, I made as much as a Sergeant in the States. I was never promoted. There were only four beauticians, two on each shift: Stella Piesecki and Norma Rose; and Rose Jenich and myself. So who needed another boss? The only thrill I got from being in charge was being the "big shot" who attended the meetings with the PX officers and filling out the orders for our supplies. Big deal!

Spiders, spiders, spiders! Their large, round, hairy bodies and long legs lurked in the ceilings of our barracks. At night you could hear them scurrying around and occasionally one would drop down on an unsuspecting person in the top bunk. One of the marines gave me his camouflage net, which I tied over my bed for protection. I don't think they were harmful, but they certainly were scary!

President Roosevelt died while I was stationed there, and seeing the flag at half-mast was a solemn sight as I went to work each day.

We had very few liberties, but I did travel the Pali Pass. As luck would have it, our car lost its brakes which was quite frightening. Thankfully, we made it safely to the bottom of the mountain and eventually back to base in one piece!

The various departments had their fun-filled cookout beach parties, which lasted all day and early evenings.

It was a thrill watching the V-J day parade in Honolulu and I wished I had been asked to participate. With all the excitement, our group of three Women Marines were oblivious to the advances of the local boys in the pressing crowds. Thankfully, Lt. Talbot, USN, came to our rescue, stood in back of us and encircled us with his arms so we could watch the parade without hassle.

I will always cherish my memories of my eight months of Ewa duty, but perhaps the one that altered my life so drastically happened the weekend of May 26-27, 1945. I was checking our barracks bulletin board and saw a notice inviting WRs to visit with the Fifth Marine survivors of Iwo Jima, who were at Camp Tarawa, Hilo, Hawaii, for R&R (Rest and Rehabilitation).

I ran up the stairs and persuaded my friend, Marian Morse, to sign up with me. We were both happy to see our names posted, along with one WR officer, Lt. Ballard, and eighteen other WRs. Our schedule looked busy but exciting, with a beach barbecue, dance, and tour of the island.

Maxine Cardinal's 21st birthday with Lowenthal, Jones and Brady

Corky, "Rosy" Roselott and Maxine Cardinal

Corky, John Thomas, Maxine Cardinal on LST 240

Lt. Talbot, USN

Women Marines from MCAS-#61
outside Chapel, Hilo, Hawaii, May 26-27, 1945

Barracks #2, Ewa, Oahu, Hawaii

Chapter Five

Absorbed in my thoughts, I was surprised to hear the pilot announcing our final approach to Newark Airport.

"There she is," I said excitedly to the attendant pushing my wheelchair as I spied Susan, smiling and waving through the glass partition. Amidst hugs and kisses, Susan asked, "Ready for your big adventure, Mother?"

Unwavering in my answer, I replied, "Oh yes, but I sure am hungry. It's almost two hours past my six o'clock dinner time."

"I think we should check into the hotel first. I'm sure they will have a restaurant. I'm hungry, too," she said.

"What time did you arrive, Susan?"

"Not much before you. I took the wrong exit somewhere, so it took a little longer than I had anticipated. Burlington is quite a distance from here, you know."

"Yes, and I really appreciate what you are doing for me," I said, giving her a kiss on the cheek.

After retrieving my baggage and her car, we checked the directions to the hotel where Dick had reserved our room. It wasn't far, but we were surprised the small restaurant was closed. It wasn't easy finding a place to eat, but eventually we found a fast food restaurant where Susan, a vegetarian, feasted on a salad while I had a cheeseburger.

The next morning, I awakened very early, showered, dressed, and was putting the finishing touches to my make-up when Susan knocked on the bathroom door.

"Too nervous to sleep, Mother?" she asked.

"Excited, not nervous," I replied, bouncing into the bedroom.

While Susan showered and dressed, I watched the news. The record heat wave sweeping across the United States was not going to let up today or tomorrow. There wasn't much news of interest taking place locally, nor worldwide. Later, as we left the parking lot, Susan heaved a sigh and remarked, "Thank goodness we have a good air conditioner, look at that unusually high temperature displayed on the car's monitor." Glancing over, I saw 98 degrees displayed as the temperature inside the car. By the time we found our route, the car was comfortably cool.

Susan and I hadn't been together for at least a year or more, so we were enjoying our visit.

"Thanks again, Susan, for driving down from Burlington and meeting my plane."

"My pleasure," she replied.

Traffic was light as we headed toward Hackettstown. We gazed out at the beautiful areas and saw the small neighborhoods awakening to a new day. The workers were beginning their trips to work and people were walking their dogs. I was sure that none of them were experiencing the kind of excitement that was flowing throughout my body.

"Isn't it amazing, Susan? Ever since computers were invented, I have been so critical and skeptical of them. Now, to me, they are really the catalyst for this incredible adventure." I couldn't stop talking. "If Jeanne hadn't been so enthusiastic and insistent about finding information concerning those three names on the flag, none of this would be happening."

The Internet, Google, or whatever she searched in December 2007 for information about the Fifth Marine Division has supplied us with the address and phone number for Leonard J. Mooney. Sadly, she found nothing about Lonnie Crowell or Gene Marshall.

"You know," I continued, "it took me a few days to get the courage to call! There were too many 'what ifs' racing through my mind. What if he was married, what if he had a jealous wife, what if he wasn't interested in a Woman Marine from yesteryear, or what if he was in poor health and couldn't communicate?"

During the ride, I recounted how I had put my fears aside and called Leonard on January 6, 2008. I had been somewhat relieved when no one answered. I left a message instead.

Months later on April 5, after receiving no response, I sat down and wrote a letter. I enclosed three photos taken the weekend of May 26-27, 1945, so he would know it was no hoax. I mailed the letter and waited.

Months, and then a year, passed with no response.

I put the flag away and the following year discarded several photos of that weekend, and pondered as to where I should send the flag.

Sometimes fate steps in and makes things happen. Two years later, on January 28, 2010, I was stunned when I answered my phone. I heard a voice ask for me by name, and then asked, "Are you the Woman Marine who contacted Leonard J. Mooney two years ago? I am his nephew, Richard Rogers, Sr."

He went on to explain that Uncle Leonard was ninety-seven years old and in poor health from a stroke. He had given Dick some stuff to separate and then dispose of unnecessary items. Dick had found my letter! How fortunate Leonard had kept it.

We must have talked for an hour or more as he explained events surrounding his Uncle's life. Mr. Mooney had been a radioman in the Fifth Marine Division, 28th Marines and Easy Company. He had witnessed his friends raising the Stars and Stripes on Mt. Suribachi. Twice! The first time they used a small flag and were photographed by Lou Lowery, a Marine and photographer for Leatherneck Magazine. The second time they used a larger flag and Leonard stood next to photographer Joe Rosenthal as he took the picture which has become so famous. He also was one of the lucky survivors of Iwo Jima who walked off the island after the Japanese were defeated.

After the war, he became a loan officer in a bank, and married Dick's aunt, Helen Domeraski, a widow with two sons, Roger and Vincent. Roger died very young in an automobile accident. He and Helen had one son, Leonard, Jr.

Dick described him as a modest, shy gentleman who never talked about the war. He had discovered his Uncle's tour of duty on Iwo Jima when a friend told him about seeing his Uncle's name in a book titled *IWO*, by Richard Wheeler, an Easy Company, Fifth Marine brother. He asked if I'd like a copy of the book, as he had several, and my quick response was yes.

I told Dick the story of how I had received the flag and how my daughter Jeanne had found Mr. Mooney's name and phone number. Before hanging up, he promised to call someday from Leonard's room at the nursing home so that we could visit via a speakerphone. I promised to mail the flag to him in care of Dick's office address, Rogers Rentals, Inc., 139 Route 46, Hackettstown, New Jersey, 07840.

(On February 1, 2010, my mission was completed, and the flag now is in the right hands to be disposed of as they deem fit. Hopefully it will be in the Marine Museum at Quantico, Virginia.)

Now I was heading in a car to meet Leonard and Dick in person.

"I've been wondering what Mr. Mooney would be like," Susan remarked. "Do you have any pictures of him?"

"Not with me, but Dick took some with the flag and sent them. He's quite handsome, for ninety-seven, and has a twinkle in his eyes when he smiles. He looks tall, even though he's sitting. Dick also sent pictures of him as a Marine, and like most Marines, he's very trim looking, even in fatigues and a helmet. Dick said this is a famous photograph, perhaps used for publicity. There are eight men in the picture, taken at Camp Pendleton ten months before the battle of Iwo Jima. Three of them, I discovered, were killed in action, three were wounded and evacuated, and Leonard was one of the two lucky ones.

"Dick sent me so many pictures and interesting articles about Easy Company of the 28th Marines. They were so fortunate to have had such an endearing Company Commander, by the name of Captain David E. Severance, who retired as a Colonel. The records he kept and the information he has shared with 'his boys' goes beyond the call of duty. After all these years, they still receive a Christmas greeting with news he has received about their buddies throughout the year! A kindred spirit?

"In one of the information sheets he had sent to Leonard, I found that Lonnie Crowell had died in 1979, and Gene Marshall in 1987. Sad news to me, because now I knew I would never be able to identify which Marine in my photo was Lonnie.

"My call from Leonard and Dick finally came on April 23, 2010. I had been preparing myself and had been jotting down questions and bits of information, but when the call came, I was so nervous I forgot all about it.

"Dick remarked that Leonard was having a good day, and was as anxious as I was to visit via the speakerphone. Dick had warned me that his speech and memory had been affected by the stroke. It didn't interfere with our visit, though.

"Leonard told me about his family and asked about mine. When I asked if he remembered anything about Crowell or Marshall, or signing the flag, his answer was, no, except he knew he had signed a flag or flags. He didn't remember the Women Marines visiting either, and I had to admit I didn't remember much, but I had pictures and information sheets in my scrapbook.

I told him how happy I was to meet him and hoped the flag hadn't brought back unpleasant memories. He assured me he was fine, and thanked me. We happily signed off with our 'Semper Fi Marine.'

"Dick and I had a short visit, and he told me Leonard had talked more than he thought he would. "'We'll call again, Maxine,' he had said.

"The next day, I received an email from Dick. 'You really perked up Uncle Leonard yesterday. We haven't seen him this happy and alert in a long time.'

"Susan, I had to laugh when I read that. Aren't people aware that's how Marines affect one another? We really are kindred spirits! I am so happy you and Dick were able to make this visit happen.

"It will be so exciting to talk to both of them in person," I said as we continued down the highway.

(L to R) Leonard J. Mooney and Dick Rogers

Chapter Six

"Well, this looks like a quaint and friendly village," said Susan, pointing to a sign. "Hackettstown, New Jersey."

"It's time for breakfast," I said. "Let's eat."

"Surely there will be one of those friendly family cafes. Oh, there it is! Stella's Kitchen. Home-Cooked Meals."

The food was delicious. Coffee was hot and perfectly brewed. The eggs, pancakes, and hash-browns never tasted better. All the personnel were friendly and made us feel so welcome. It had been a wise decision.

Exiting the cafe, I turned to Susan. "I need to take Leonard a gift. You have that beautiful decanter of Vermont Maple Syrup for the Rogers. I just can't think of what would be suitable."

As we headed for the car, we stopped in two small gift shops, but found nothing. We thought of a few military things, but that didn't seem right, nor did a book. We returned to the car and started down Main Street.

"I have it!" I said excitedly. I turned to Susan and explained, "During World War II, the Woman Marines had a red rose named for them. I'll get him a Lady Marine Red Rose! What could be more appropriate? Let's find a florist."

Susan parked the car, retrieved her purse from the backseat, and removed her I-Phone. She found a florist one block away. A sign on the front window read, 'On Vacation.' I was heartbroken.

"Don't panic, Mother, let's see if we can find another," Susan quietly said.

She finally found a Bridal and Florist Shop and, getting the directions, we were soon welcomed into a fantasy world. The shop was so professionally decorated, it looked like a movie scene. I explained to the clerk what I wanted and why. She soon emerged from the back room with the most beautiful, velvety-looking red rose surrounded by small white baby's breath and fern.

"This is so beautiful!" I exclaimed to the clerk as she began wrapping it in several sheets of clear plastic. "Thank you." I looked at Susan. "Yes, this is the perfect gift from a Woman

Marine to her hero from Iwo."

As we entered the car, Susan said, "Isn't technology quite wonderful, Mother? A few flips on my iPhone and your problem was solved."

Once again, I had to admit she was correct.

Red rose given by Maxine Wehry to Leonard J. Mooney

Chapter Seven

As we continued our quest to find Rogers' Rentals, Inc., I told Susan about the volunteers I served with in the Hospice/Bereavement/Palliative Care Unit at Bay Pines VA Medical Center who had tried to help find information regarding the three names, and who were encouraging me to write the story.

Bonnie Hosse and her late husband Ed, a Marine survivor of the Chosin Reservoir in Korea, were both from Evansville, Indiana. She tried to find Lonnie Crowell's name in some of her telephone directories, but found no listing, nor anyone who knew him. She was disappointed by not being able to help a Marine from Indiana.

Pam Hinds Pajac and her husband Joe Pajac (who had been wounded on Iwo Jima and was a Fifth Marine survivor) checked through his connections, but found only the same information as Jeanne. Pam was so enthused with the story that, as a member of Daughters of the American Revolution and one of their writers, she composed a short synopsis of the story for their Florida publication.

"Marines helping Marines," I remarked. "It's laughable, Susan, when the story circulated at the VA, some of my friends thought there was more to this trip than two Marines from World War II meeting because of a name on a Japanese flag." We both smiled, and I continued. "I also have to give credit to the Gulfport Senior Center's Writer's Workshop members. They have really encouraged me to write it as a memoir for my family, but felt it had an element of being historical also. With tongue in cheek, I had said, 'Hysterical might be a better word.'"

We drove in silence for a while, and I began daydreaming about how great it would have been if all three Marines had been found and the four of us could share this day.

"I need your help, Mother, I think we're almost there. We need Route 46 and Johnson Road. The number is 139. Here are the directions."

We turned onto Route 46, and I began checking numbers on the buildings.

"It should be the next street, Susan. Dick said to turn left into the parking lot and his office is next door."

Susan turned left, not into a parking lot, but onto the street.

As I surveyed all the large semis and trailers to my right, I stammered, "I – I don't think this is where we are to park."

Returning to the corner, we spied Dick standing in the parking lot. He looked exactly like the pictures he had sent of himself with Mr. Mooney and the flag I had mailed.

"Welcome to Hackettstown and Rogers' Rentals," he said as we left the comfort of our air conditioned automobile to face the unbearable heat. He smiled and gave each of us a hug. "So happy you could come. It will mean so much to Uncle Leonard. Leave your car here, Susan, and we'll return after our visit. I'll give you a tour of my business and the area before we head for Warren Haven, where Leonard awaits his guests."

"This is my home base of the three locations I have. Number two is in Greenville, Pennsylvania, and number three is in Hazelton, Pennsylvania."

He pointed to a large area of the lot. "See all those refrigerated trailers assembled there? They are filled with M&M candies, ready for shipment throughout the world. In case you weren't aware, Hackettstown is the home of Mars' M&M factory. I have a few copies of a book by Joel Glenn Brenner entitled 'The Emperors of Chocolate – Inside The Secret World of Hershey and Mars'. It's very interesting. I'll give each of you a copy before you leave."

"Gee, thanks," we said, almost in unison.

After our tour of the business facility, Dick escorted us into one of his 1991 Fleetwood Brougham Cadillacs.

"Luxurious," I said.

"These are the last of the big Caddies with rear wheel drive. The Big Boats," he remarked. "I collect them." He then told us the interesting stories of how and where he had found his prized possessions.

What a wonderful tour guide he was, as he explained how Hackettstown supposedly evolved from a glacier. Named for a gentleman, Samuel Hackett, it is a small town of approximately ten thousand people, and was incorporated in 1853. Primarily it had been a farming community, but like so many areas, its countryside has been transformed into subdivisions.

Driving through the beautiful hills and valleys on winding tree-lined two-way highways, we forgot all about the unusual heat wave. We were soon reminded, however, as we arrived at the Rogers' home and found Susan, his wife, loading boxes into her SUV. Rolling down the windows in our car, we hurriedly spent a few minutes of hellos before continuing our tour.

"Because of this sweltering heat wave, we were reluctant to bring Uncle Leonard to our home for lunch," Dick explained. "Susan is bringing it to Warren Haven."

"I'm sorry she has to go to all that trouble, Dick. We could have gone out later."

"Oh, no, Maxine, Leonard is looking forward to having company for lunch. We can't disappoint him, can we?"

"I suppose not. I'd be disappointed, too. I'm really looking forward to meeting him. It is great meeting you and Susan, also. So happy you helped arrange all of this. Thank you."

From the backseat, Susan interjected, "One thing I'm sure of, these two old Marines are going to have an unbelievable get-together today. I'm glad I'm here to see it."

Bonnie and Ed Hosse, Evansville, IN

Frieda Story and Maxine Wehry
VAMC Hospice / Bereavement 5C, Bay Pines, FL, 2011

Chapter Eight

"Well, here we are," Dick announced. "This is Warren Haven, a government assisted living facility. It is owned and operated by Warren County. It's the best in our area."

If someone had asked me how I felt when I arrived here, I wonder how I would have answered. I was meeting a man whose only attachment to me was a name, barely visible on a souvenir Japanese Rising Sun flag. Perhaps if I hadn't already spoken to him, nor seen a photo of him, I would have been more apprehensive and less enthusiastic. As it was, I think, I felt I was meeting an old Marine friend from the past, and was so fortunate to have this opportunity that my happiness was almost a teenage giddiness.

As we entered the building, we were met by one of the staff. "Marcy, this is Maxine, who came all the way from Florida to see Leonard, and this is her daughter, Susan," Dick said.

Marcy, who looked so pleasant and had a beautiful smile as she acknowledged us, asked, "Oh, is this the lady you told us about?"

"Yes," Dick replied, "she's the one who sent the flag, and all of that."

"Oh, welcome! Your story was so interesting. I really enjoyed hearing all about it. Everyone here knows about you. Glad you could come. Enjoy your visit."

"Thank you. I'm sure we will."

"Nice meeting you," she said, still beaming.

"Nice meeting you also," Susan and I responded.

As we started to walk down the corridor toward her office, she said we would find Leonard at the end of the hall to our left. With a smile and a wave of her hand, she entered the door.

Dick glanced at me. "Are you excited?"

I answered quickly, "Excited! I can't wait!"

As we approached Leonard, Dick asked, "Where are the Marines?"

I retorted, "Did they all leave town when they heard Maxine was coming?"

"That's right," I heard him say.

Susan and Dick could be heard laughing in the background.

I stepped in front of his wheelchair. A handsome man with a smile on his face and a twinkle in his eyes sat facing me. I placed the rose in his hand and said, "A Lady Marine Red Rose for my hero from Iwo," then gave him a hug and a kiss. "So good to meet you Leonard. How are you?" I asked, patting him on the back.

"I'm fine, and good to meet you too. Is this for me?" he asked, pointing to the rose.

"Yes, it's yours," I said, and explained about the Lady Marine Red Rose of World War II. "I thought this was the most appropriate gift I could bring to you, my hero from Iwo."

Dick had told me he didn't consider himself a hero, but to me, all servicemen were heroes.

"Thank you," he said.

I'd almost bet this was the first rose he had ever received from a woman, let alone a Woman Marine. I should have asked him.

He glanced up at me and said, "I thought you would be old," then hesitated. "You're older." Then, shaking his head and repeating, "No, no, no," he waved his hands, as if he wanted to erase his words.

"I am old," I said, ignoring his frustration. "After all, we were only twenty-one back there on that beach."

"Oh no, not me," he said, with a sly as-a-fox expression on his face.

"I know, you were thirty-one."

"Yeah."

"Closer to thirty-two," Dick interjected from behind us.

"Leonard, this is my daughter, Susan," I said, putting my arm around her shoulders.

"Nice to meet you, dear. Give me a hand," he said, extending his.

"I will as soon as I e taking your picture for a moment." Offering her hand, she said, "So nice meeting you. I've been hearing all about you." Pointing towards me, she continued, "You're kinda making her day."

"I'm glad, and I'm happy to see her, too." His smile seemed so genuine.

"We don't remember if we ever met before today, but this is just great." Holding and patting his hand, I said, "I am so happy to be here."

"You're in good shape, too," he remarked.

"Thank you. I couldn't have made this trip to meet everyone if I wasn't. You're in good shape, too, Leonard."

"Yes, I guess I am."

"You're in better shape than some fifty year olds. I see a lot of them at the VA, it's sad."

He looked so sorry. "I'm so thankful I'm not that bad."

"For your age, Leonard, you are great. I may not reach ninety-seven, but if I do, I hope I wear my age as well."

"Yeah, and I have my own teeth, too," he quipped.

I should have added, "Me too."

Dick interrupted us. "Let's go to the visitor's lounge, where we can relax, sit down and visit."

"Good idea, I agree," Susan said, and turned off her camera.

Dick pushed Leonard back down the hall to the lounge. It was so tastefully decorated and had such a warm comfortable aura surrounding it. Soft lighting came from the table lamps. Several chairs and couches had been placed in clusters around the room for convenient and intimate visiting. The walls displayed some beautiful pictures, but what was outstanding was a beautiful stained glass creation, which enhanced the rear wall. Nearby was a round oak table, where we decided to sit. Dick placed his papers, books, and files on the table. Susan went searching for a suitable vase for the rose.

As Leonard and I sat facing one another with happy, smiling faces, our demeanor was such, you would have thought we'd been acquainted for years.

"How was your trip?" he asked.

I told him about the storm in Tampa and how frightened I had been flying through the dark clouds into the sunny clear skies and a smooth flight. Laughing, I said, "I'm not an avid flier, but nothing was going to spoil my trip to meet you—not even that zigzagging lightning.

"Dick's choice of a hotel for us last night was a good one. It wasn't far away, so easy to find, clean and comfortable. The drive from Newark to Hackettstown was delightful."

Susan returned and placed the vase with the rose on the table.

"Very nice, thank you, dear," Leonard said softly.

"You're welcome. Sorry I interrupted your conversation."

Dick, checking his camera, said, "No problem."

Leonard began talking. "My sergeant was from Florida."

"Oh, is that right?"

"Yeah, Boots, Boots…" He then became so frustrated when he couldn't remember his last name. "You can see it there," he said to Dick, pointing to some papers.

"Crowe?" Dick asked.

"No, I didn't say anything about Crowe," he said disgustedly.

"I brought this," Dick said, holding up several sheets of white paper stapled together to form a book.

"Oh, good, from Captain…"

"Severance," Dick added.

"My Captain. He's something else. He sends news all the time to everyone. Still does." You could tell by the tone of his voice Leonard had great admiration for his Captain, friend, and fellow Marine.

"Dick told me all about him when we spoke on the phone, and sent me several of the communications you have received over the years, also, several photos. I may have that list, unless it's a newer one."

Leonard started to smile. I wish I could have understood the story completely, because there was something about the President. This is how he related it to us.

"This guy sat down next to me. He said I had to get up for the President. I said, 'How old are you? You mean I have to take orders from you? Well, I'm almost old enough to be your father. No!'" He said it rather emphatically.

Then he continued his story: "One time, only time, first time, I went over the hill. Two of us left together. Some of the Marines told my sergeant, 'Mooney's gone — he won't be back.'"

"'He'll be back, don't kid yourself, want to put some money on it?'"

"'Yeah, yeah,' they yelled."

"'Then put it right there,'" said Leonard and slammed his hand on the table to mimic his sergeant.

"I came — "

"You came back, didn't you?" I said.

"They said, 'Your sergeant is something else. He put money on you.'" Leonard remarked, "He must have thought I was all right."

He continued his story and I couldn't put it together. He formed the f-word a couple of times, and mentioned something about fifteen or thirty.

In jest, I quickly asked, "Hours or days?"

He talked about a plane and no greens, but he sat all day and tried to hitchhike a ride back, but trucks — trucks — trucks kept passing by. Someone must have stopped because Dick, who knew the whole story from when Leonard could relate it, chimed in:

"Mr. Gallo picked you up, Mr. Gallo, from the winery."

"Yeah, he took me to dinner and back to the base. They lived in tents up there, and everyone saw me coming. 'Boy, Mooney, you're going to get it,' they chorused."

"Sergeant sent me to the Captain. 'You have to go to the Colonel.'"

"'Oh, oh,' I thought. When I got there, the line was so long, I was almost the last one! I stood there like a rock. I had my story all ready for him."

"He gave a good line of bull is what he did," Dick said.

"He must have thought I was all right. He only gave me fifteen minutes of outside work."

"Fifteen minutes for AWOL?" I couldn't believe it!

"My Captain said I would have to do half again of that time and when I started to explain, he said he didn't want to hear my story either!"

"We had some good officers in there, but some not so good," I remarked.

"Yeah, but I had good ones," he said proudly, then began to chuckle.

We laughed with him, knowing we had awakened a happy

memory in a mind weakened by the stroke.

I was still having a hard time with that fifteen minutes. Was it because they were heading to Iwo Jima? Most ended up in the brig for that. Dick, still looking through the list, asked, "Boots was Wells, right?"

Frustrated, Leonard replied, "No, isn't there a sergeant in there?"

"I should go get my book from the car," Dick said. "His name is Boots, he was wounded, returned from the hospital ship, and was killed."

"You saw a lot of that, didn't you, Leonard?"

He covered his face. "Yes," he said. "I felt so bad."

"It wasn't your fault," I commented.

"I prayed all the time. I guess it wasn't my time."

40 man patrol from E Company, Suribachi Yama, Iwo Jima, 1945

He straddled this during battle, 1945 - Revisited 2002

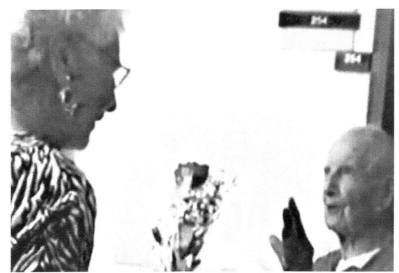

Maxine Cardinal Wehry presents rose to Leonard J. Mooney

Leonard J. Mooney and Dave Severance

Chapter Nine

"Boots, Boots, Boots," Leonard kept repeating. It seemed it was very important for him to remember his sergeant's last name.

I started telling him about another boy from Indiana, whose name and address I had found on the list Dick had sent me. He was from a town, Sullivan, which was perhaps thirty miles north of my hometown. The pictures I had from Marine Beach, Hilo, Hawaii had the notation "boys from Indiana" on the back, and I was now wondering if this marine could be on the picture with Lonnie Crowell and me.

"Here's something interesting I brought for you to read," Dick said. "It's a true story, or at least they say it's true. It's about Jim Bradley, the son of John Bradley, the Navy Corpsman who helped raise the flag on Mt. Suribachi. It's a good read."

I was looking at it when Dick excitedly announced: "Thomas! 'Boots Thomas.' I knew I'd remember."

"Oh, baby, that's him, 'Boots Thomas.'" Leonard exclaimed.

"He was quite a guy, his sergeant. So was Mike Strank, 'Big Mike' from Pittsburgh."

Leonard was listening so intently, then he looked at me so seriously. "Do you know what was wrong with him? His feet, he had really bad feet. I don't know how he ever got in the Marines, but his legs were strong and he could really march!" Using his arms, he demonstrated the swiftness of his sergeant, whom I'm sure he admired in spite of the difference in their ages.

"Okay," Dick interrupted, "for the record, while you're on camera, here are your original pictures. I promised I'd return them to you, but I made copies of them."

I picked up the three pictures. "Well, I had forgotten I had a picture of me with those two boys." Holding it for Leonard to see, I pointed to the Marine on my right. "I think this is Lonnie Crowell."

Susan came over to check which one I had pointed out, just as I asked Leonard, "Do you think that could be Lonnie Crowell?"

"Could be, I know his name and him, but don't know for sure."

To Dick, he said, "I told you."

Dick said, "Yes, we think it's Lonnie Crowell."

As I checked the picture of the man on the beach playing the clarinet, I noticed Leonard seemed to be studying it also.

"Did you know Crowe?" he asked.

"No, it was Lonnie Crowell who gave me the flag."

I learned later Crowe had been called "Music Man," so perhaps the young Marine on the beach was Crowe.

"Now this is my girlfriend, Marion Morse," I said, pointing to the girl in the picture with me. "Oh my, I have a bathing suit on!" I was shocked. I didn't remember this picture at all. It looked as if I had a beer in my hand. Must have been a prop! I didn't even like beer.

Susan and Dick started laughing. "Did you think you were nude?" Dick asked.

"No," I said, laughing. "I'm just surprised I had a bathing suit on. These two boys in the picture with me were on the beach in khakis. I had a picture of them in my collection, but when I hadn't heard from Leonard, I threw most of them away because I doubted my family would want them or the flag." (Periodically, I have been discarding pictures and items that were meaningful to me, but would be nothing but junk to my family after I depart this world.)

I mentioned the boy from Sullivan, Roudebush. Leonard became alert.

"Yeah, I knew him well, we were close friends. He was a big guy, really big."

"Do you think either of these boys in the picture could be him?" Leonard shook his head. "Don't know."

(After visiting Leonard, I spoke with Roudebush, but he couldn't remember Leonard and said he wasn't a big man. Checking the list of living members of the Easy Company, I discovered a Marine by the name of Robert E. Rodebaugh, from Bartlesville, Oklahoma. Could Leonard be confused by the similarity of their names?)

"Oh," I remarked. "I found our schedule for that weekend. We really weren't with those boys too much!"

"You told me a day or so," Dick replied.

"Neither were we," Leonard chimed in. I should have asked him where they went. Japan?

Dick picked up a long envelope and I recognized it as the one I had put the flag in to mail to Leonard.

"Oh, there it is," I exclaimed.

"I'm unveiling the flag for the record," Dick explained as he looked toward the camera.

My heart was racing wildly and I glanced at the solemn face of Leonard. Dick had already told me that Leonard wasn't upset seeing it, but I felt sure it had to bring back unpleasant memories.

"Did Leonard find his name?"

"Yes, but it was hard to find."

"I know, and I still believe those spots are blood." It stands to reason they could be; after the war, I believe, it was listed as the bloodiest battle in the Pacific. Or was it just the Marine Corps? Anyway, no doubt that black sand of Iwo Jima turned red.

Susan and Dick kept busy taking photographs. "Say 'cheese,'" they both said.

"Cheese," Leonard said, "and with my own teeth too!" We all laughed. He did have a sense of humor.

"We have to get a picture of Leonard and me together holding the flag," I declared. "After all, this piece of silk is what brought us together for this sensational celebration."

Leonard's chair was positioned close to mine, and he smiled. Susan, who had moved his chair, remarked, "You didn't know you'd be so photographed, did you?"

I'm not sure how many poses of this were taken, but several. Leonard featured one on his Christmas card of December 2010. Along with his newsletter, he explained my presence. For two old Marines, we looked fantastic. With all that notoriety, Leonard, I felt like a celebrity. Thank you!

Maxine Cardinal and Marion Morse
with 2nd Battalion 5th Marines, Hilo, Hawaii, 1945

"Music Man", Marine Beach, Hilo, Hawaii, 1945

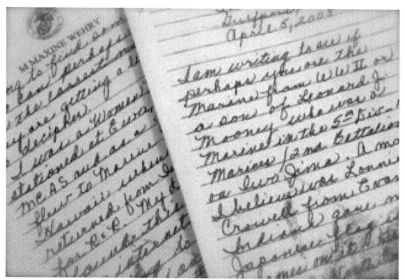

Original letter from Maxine Cardinal Wehry to Leonard J. Mooney

Maxine Cardinal Wehry and Leonard J. Mooney

Chapter Ten

"The flag is still in pretty good shape, isn't it," I commented as Dick refolded it.

"Yes," he replied, "you took good care of it all those years. The camera's still on," he continued, "let's hear the story of the flag,"

"Well, I received it from Lonnie Crowell the weekend of May 26-27, 1945, when a group of Women Marines visited the survivors of Iwo Jima on Marine Beach, Hilo, Hawaii." Tapping Leonard on the knee, I remarked, "Oh boy, sixty-five years ago, but we're still young."

"I'm glad I'm here," Leonard said.

"Me too, and I'm glad we finally got together. You signed that flag, along with Gene Marshall from North Carolina, and Lonnie Crowell from Evansville, Indiana. He's the one who gave the flag to me. I never saw him again, and never corresponded with him. All I had was this flag, stored away with other World War II memorabilia. Then on July 14, 1999, I discovered those fading names on it."

Dick showed a picture to Leonard, who said, "Where'd you get that?"

"It was yours, and I had it enlarged."

"Which one is me?"

"Neither, I'm not sure, but I think this is Lonnie Crowell," he said, and handed the picture to me.

"This one definitely looks like one of the boys," I said.

Dick and I differed on which one looked like Lonnie. He gave me the benefit of the doubt, but then, almost apologetically, I remarked that it is hard to distinguish people when they are all dressed alike. We finally decided it could be neither.

Dick handed me a photograph album to view.

"Oh," I said, "I have my picture taken with him too," as I spied the Commandant of the Marine Corps, General James J. Jones.

"Leonard met him on his first trip to Iwo," Dick remarked.

We enjoyed looking at all the pictures displayed in the album. It made Dick's narration all the more interesting.

"I knew Leonard had been in the military," he began, "as had all men his age, but I didn't know that he was in the Marines or any of that until a friend of mine told me about his name being in a book he read, and brought it to me. Its title is *IWO* and it was written by Richard Wheeler. Wheeler was in his outfit, his platoon, as a matter of fact. He died about a year and a half ago.

"I asked Leonard about this," Dick continued. "He said that, yeah, he had been a Marine on Iwo and saw the flags raised, but then he clammed up on me, changed the subject and asked about my parents and the weather. Over the years, we never mentioned it, except for dribs and drabs.

"Then one Christmas, I stopped in for a holiday drink and noticed a Christmas greeting and letter from Colonel Severance. 'You can have that,' Leonard told me, so I started reading it.

"Hey, we can go to Iwo," I said.

"'You can, I went once and I'm not going back.'"

"'Let's go,' I kept saying. 'I'll take you. It won't cost you anything,' but he wouldn't change his mind. I decided I'd call his commanding officer and see if he was going. 'No,' he told me, 'I know just how Leonard feels. I'm not over the Japanese yet, but don't pay any attention to me. I'll get it all set up, don't worry about a thing.'

"I told him, "I won't go unless Leonard goes. I'll get back with you.'

"Then, a couple of weeks later, in between drinks on one of those heavy drinking days, Leonard told me he'd think about going."

Interjecting, I said, "You're a drinker, Leonard?"

"Oh yeah, Old Fashioneds, but I could handle it," Leonard said rather sheepishly.

Laughing, I said, "Well, I didn't know Marines drank."

Everyone chuckled as Dick said, "He could whack 'em down sometimes. In fact, that night he wanted me to have one for the road, but I still had to drive home. It wouldn't have been the smart thing to do. I was happy he was at least going to think about going. I assured him again I would take care of everything. I had no idea what we were getting into. I figured, we'd get on an airplane, fly to Iwo, see some sights, take some pictures, walk up the black sandy beach to where the flags were raised, and fly home. Nothing could have been further from the truth. That's how naive I was. As you can see, he agreed to go, and that album holds the pictures of a 'trip of a lifetime.' I've been around, but this was it. Uncle Leonard, my wife, Susan, who is a nurse, and I returned home tired but awestruck by what we had seen and experienced."

Leonard sat almost motionless as Dick began the saga of their trip. I watched with compassion the various expressions on his face, and wondered which trip he was remembering: February-March 1945, or March 2002?

Apparently, after Leonard decided to go on the Reunion Honor Flight, Dick's fears had bordered on the bizarre. He thought they would be living in huts out in the jungle, surrounded by wild animals, snakes and bugs, with no modern bath facilities and swampy—similar, perhaps, to Florida's Lake Okeechobee. "I know they thought I was some kind of a nut, with all my calls and questions," he explained as he began to narrate their next stops on Guam, Saipan, Tinian, and Iwo Jima.

The Reunion Honor Flight, as Dick called it, had made all their reservations and everything ran smoothly as they traveled from New Jersey to Los Angeles, where they met the other group that was going. From there, they flew to Hawaii, and bad luck presented its ugly head: One of them had a seat near the front, one in the back, and one somewhere else.

"Leonard, at age 89, even though in fairly good health, became anxious not having one of us with him. I didn't like it either," Dick remarked. He went to the counter, explained the situation, but got nowhere.

I would say Dick became a little assertive and asked to speak to the manager, who gave him the same story, 'It's a full flight and we can't switch seats.'

"Well," Dick said, "I told him I could just see this big headline in the newspaper, 'Air Line Treated an Iwo Jima Veteran—'."

"'Hold on, sir, and let me check,' the manager said.

"We had no more trouble, and the three of us ended up sitting together."

That brought laughter from everyone.

"When I called Leonard to ask if he had a passport, he questioned why he needed one. 'Didn't need one the last time I was there,' he had retorted. I explained to him we had returned the island of Iwo to Japan in nineteen sixty-nine, so perhaps that was the reason.

"We landed on Guam late at night and were surprised to find such a modern airport, and a customs office. The customs agent asked where we were headed, and I told him, eventually, Iwo Jima. I explained we were with the Reunion Honor Flight because Leonard was a Marine survivor of that battle, and had witnessed the flag raising on Mt. Suribachi as a member of the Fifth Marine Division's Easy Company.

"He stopped dead in his tracks," Dick related. "He found a piece of paper and, retrieving his pen, asked for Leonard's autograph. Then wanted his picture taken with him.

"From that moment on, wherever he went, it was the same ritual, even though Leonard kept repeating, 'I was only a Marine PFC, radioman with the Fifth Marine Division, 28th Marines, 2nd Battalion and Easy Company. I didn't help raise the flags, I was just there when my buddies did it!'"

"It didn't make any difference to those people on the islands," Dick said. "They think the sun rises and sets on the rear ends of those World War II veterans."

Susan and Dick took the two-day side trips to Saipan and Tinian, while Leonard, as Dick tells it, stayed on Guam, "hangin' around the hotel pool where the food, booze, and beautiful bikini-clad females were."

"You'll find his picture in the album somewhere and can see for yourself how much he enjoyed it," he said, laughing.

Pointing to a photo we were observing, Dick advised us the two ships anchored a distance offshore on Saipan or Tinian were fully equipped for battle. Food, ammunition, tanks, guns, jeeps were all on board, enough for a Division. Troops could be added quickly.

"When we arrived on Saipan," Dick related, "we looked like bums and were really embarrassed. We had dressed for traipsing through the bush and countryside. The welcoming committee, however, were dressed to the nines! Several of them circulated throughout our group, collecting information concerning the veterans or the family members.Their knowledge was parlayed into their speeches during the ceremony.

"We did dress more suitably for the dinner and ceremony," he added, "and each guest received a medal honoring their visit. They included one for Leonard. Those people were so friendly and accommodating," Dick remarked. "They couldn't have been any nicer."

Susan and I were enjoying the photo album filled with pictures from Saipan and Tinian. I can't remember which island featured an area where inhabitants seemed to migrate when committing suicide by jumping from the cliff to the rocks and water below. One of the Japanese Admirals, who was embarrassed by losing his ship in the war, went there and committed hari-kari. Suicide, it seems, pervades the world.

The two photos most memorable to me were a group of Marines going through maneuvers, and the World War II old amphib entrenched in the sand and water along the shoreline–a remnant and grim reminder of the war.

At the time, I wondered where those Marines might be headed. Never thought to ask Dick if he knew. Now, as I'm writing this, I realize those pictures had been taken in 2002 and 2005, so perhaps they have seen action in Iraq or Afghanistan.

"All the Islands were beautiful and the people were so friendly," Dick commented, "and even though they have been rebuilt and improved, bunkers are still visible everywhere."

"Perhaps the inhabitants are oblivious to their existence," I said, "and the bunkers are invisible to them as they picnic and frolic in the sand and water. Sure hope so," I added.

"We arrived back on Guam after our two-day absence and called my Aunt Helen, Leonard's wife, in New Jersey. We were quite surprised my cell worked so well that many miles away. She seemed a little anxious about my call."

"'Is Leonard all right? How's he doing? Is he feeling okay?'

"I walked over to the hotel window, which overlooked the pool, just in time to see them serving Leonard a drink and a group of bathing beauties arriving.

"I had to laugh when I answered her questions. 'Oh, he's fine and right now he's feelin' Real Good!'"

"'Don't let him get into any trouble,' she cautioned before hanging up the phone.

"I thought to myself, I doubt if he does, but he could," Dick said, tongue in cheek.

We all laughed at Dick's remark and teased Leonard about his drinking and roving male eyes. Never too old to look! Reminded me of the old saying, 'Once a Marine, Always a Marine,' and at eighty-nine, I believe Leonard was still playing the role!

Dick continued, "The night before we left for Iwo Jima, they served a lavish dinner and had an interesting and entertaining ceremony. The place was filled with brass, officers from every branch of the service, and several civilian dignitaries. They presented everyone with an honor award, a souvenir of their trip.

"Afterwards, I approached General James J. Jones, USMC and asked if I could get a picture of him with my Uncle Leonard, a Fifth Marine survivor of Iwo Jima. 'He was only a PFC,' I added."

"'It would be my honor and pleasure,' General Jones replied, 'and tonight, he is a General.'"

Calling over a Marine photographer, they posed for a picture, which is perhaps an official Marine photo in the Marine archives. I would assume the two of them had a very interesting conversation regarding the battle and the flag raising on Mt. Suribachi.

At one of the Women Marine Association's Conventions, I had my picture taken with General Jones, and I feel sure Leonard treasures his photograph taken with one of our Commandants as much as I do mine.

They traveled to Iwo Jima the following day on a brand new Continental Airlines 737 or 747.

"She was a beauty! We sat in the last three seats in the rear of the plane," Dick remarked. "During the flight, one of the pilots came looking for Leonard and asked if he would sign two copies of the book *Flags Of Our Father's*, the story about the flag raising on Mt. Suribachi."

"'One is for me and the other is for my Marine son,' he explained."

"'I will be more than happy to,' Leonard responded."

Dick continued, "I questioned him whether or not the plane was on autopilot."

"'Oh no,' he replied. 'We have four Captains on board. I'm the Senior. Each of us is qualified and certified to fly these planes. This is Continental's most prestigious flight and we're here just for you.'

"He extended his hand to Leonard, thanked him for his service and the autograph, turned, and departed up the aisle. I was really impressed," Dick told us as he continued with the story.

"As we circled Iwo, Leonard began laughing.

"'What's so funny?' I asked.

"'I was remembering this incident. After we reached the top, it was so quiet, we thought it was all over up there, even though we could hear it going on below us. We found this Naval gun protruding, so I straddled it while some buddies stood around. Two of them held a Japanese flag below the barrel and others took pictures. Suddenly we heard Captain Severance yelling, 'Mooney, get your ass off that gun, there's a battle going on.'

"I jumped off real quick and yelled, 'Yessir!'"

Later that day, when they found the gun, he posed beside it. I hope it made him laugh again, not cry.

As I studied both photos, I smiled. The young, cocky, swash-buckling Marine with his helmet askew and the meek, mild-mannered, eighty-nine year old Marine, still standing tall, seemed to be two different individuals. Which one was I visiting? Pondering the question, I soon realized the man sitting next to me with a twinkle in his eyes, a mischievous grin, and a lilt of laughter in his voice at times was also a kind, soft-spoken, and mannerly person who still possessed the traits of both.

Maxine Wehry and Leonard J. Mooney

Leonard J. Mooney and Dick Rogers, Iwo Jima, 2002

Camp Pendleton, CA, 10 months before the Battle of Iwo Jima
Standing: Charles Lindberg, Dick Wheeler, Everett Lavelle,
Louie B. Adrian, Leonard J. Mooney
Kneeling: Harold Keller, Edward Krisik, Edward Romero

Chapter Eleven

Dick related a short summary of what had transpired on top of the mountain. "Leonard told me they were held up there for five days. We thought things couldn't be any worse than they had been as we inched our way to the top, but it was. We hadn't seen nothin' yet. It was hell."

There are enough books in circulation about this massacre, so I'm not going into the gory details. It's not my story and I can't relate to anything I didn't experience. My memoir is about what transpired in my life that was affected by the circumstances surrounding World War II, especially the battle of Iwo Jima, a Japanese "Rising Sun" flag, and three Marines from the Fifth Marine's Easy Company, Lonnie Crowell, Gene Marshall, and Leonard J. Mooney, my heroes from Iwo!

"As the plane was landing on Iwo," Dick continued, "an announcement was made that all veterans were to exit first. Leonard balked!

"'I'm not gettin' off,' he proclaimed.

"'Why not?'

"'I'm just not gettin' off.'

"'That's all right,' the attendant said. 'Don't pressure him. Many of the veterans have a difficult time doing this.'

"I glanced at Leonard again and asked, 'Why? What's wrong?'

"'You can't get off with me,' he replied.

"The attendant assured him we could all get off together, so we continued to the front of the plane. As the door opened, we gasped. A group of Marines were lined up, waiting to welcome us. Leonard was awestruck.

"'I think there's somebody important on here,' he whispered to me.

"'Yeah,' I said, 'you and all these other veterans,' and gave him a love pat on the back.

"'Well, I'm going down there and shake hands with every one of those damn Marines,' he said, and proceeded to do so. All the brass from the previous evening were there, along with the civilian dignitaries, and an entourage of Japanese. Leonard wouldn't even look at them."

When my daughter asked what his thoughts were when he saw them, his answer was, "I didn't want to have anything to do with them."

That's understandable, I mused. Perhaps the Japanese felt the same towards us. Anyone having gone through the horrors of war would definitely feel more animosity towards the enemy than those who only read about it.

Dick continued to narrate. "When all the Reunion of Honor ceremonies were completed, we headed for the beach. Offshore, I noticed six warships anchored, and questioned a Marine lieutenant what their presence meant. He informed us there were actually seven, but the aircraft carrier was beyond our view.

"'We're here for your safety,' he said, 'and there's also a lot of brass here, you know. Have you noticed the F-16s and F-18s flying around? There are also one thousand Marines patrolling the island making sure it is secure and there are no hidden booby traps, and planes from the aircraft carrier fly a complete perimeter of the island continuously. You will be safe here.'

"He further informed us that each veteran would be furnished a Humvee with a driver and medic aboard. If someone should become ill, they would be treated here, or if necessary, they would be flown by helicopter out to a jet and flown to Guam for further treatment. They had thought of everything.

"'How long are you here for?'

"'When you leave, we leave,' he replied.

"I tried climbing the mountain," Dick remarked, "but for every two steps up, I slid back three, and I was only carrying a camera. Its hard to comprehend how those Marines advanced to the top, when the terrain was mostly black lava sand and they were carrying their rifle, ammunition, gear and equipment. Leonard's radio alone weighed forty-five pounds. Besides that, they were surrounded by the Japanese, hiding in the caves, just waiting to annihilate as many of them as possible!

"We rode in the Humvee to the top where the monument now stands, supposedly where the flags were raised. This had to be a very emotional time for Leonard, after having fought there and witnessed the deaths of so many friends."

Dick had a picture of the monument, but I can't describe it too well. It looked very impressive, made of marble or stone. It had the Fifth Marine insignia as well as the Eagle, Globe and Anchor emblem, and a picture of the last and most famous of the flag raisings.

Dick continued, "Leonard's priority, as we planned our trip, was to visit the cemetery so he could pray for, and say goodbye to, his buddies. When we asked where the cemetery was, they informed us that all the bodies had been removed and were now buried in Arlington National Cemetery, the Punch Bowl on Oahu, and in their hometown cemeteries.

"Leonard was disappointed, but we visited the monument, placed where the cemetery had been located, and he prayed for his friends, whom he says 'are the true heroes.'

"This was a real eye-opener for me," Dick said. "I didn't know the Punch Bowl was a cemetery. It had been offered as a side trip when we first went to Iwo. I thought it was a Hawaiian Luau or party, and we opted not to go. I knew better on our second trip, and we visited it. Leonard found the grave of his best friend, Henry 'Hank' Hanson, who was killed as they fought side by side on top of the mountain in that bloody massacre. Perhaps this time he found more closure and solace, as he prayed at his friend's gravesite for him and all the others who are now resting in peace on American soil."

"So many crosses there," Leonard remarked sadly.

"Yes, Leonard, I know. Al and I visited there on our trip to the Hawaiian Islands when we celebrated our twenty-fifth wedding anniversary."

"I'm so grateful to have been a part of making his wish come true," Dick said, as he reflected on this special day for Leonard.

Their story continued. "On our first trip, I took an American flag so we could get our picture taken on Mt. Suribachi. Leonard's photo was taken a multitude of times, because when those Marines discovered he was a survivor, they were finding all sorts of things for him to autograph and then wanted their picture taken with him.

He was the star attraction of that day.

"When I asked if they had a flag, they said no. When I asked if they'd like mine, they were jubilant. One of the young Marines asked if I'd have Leonard sign it for them.

"By this time, Leonard was getting tired, and his annoyance showed in his voice as he told them, 'Don't you guys understand? I didn't raise any flag! I was only a PFC and radioman, I didn't do anything, I was just there when it happened!'

"'Yes, sir, we understand,' the young Marine uttered shyly, 'but would you please sign it anyway?'

"How could he refuse?

"We left it with them. Later I realized Leonard and I hadn't gotten our pictures taken with the flag as planned, but my memory of the happy faces on those young Marines made it all worthwhile," Dick remarked, and Leonard agreed.

"I'm confused about the flag," my daughter stated. "Was it customary for servicemen to carry their country's flag?"

"I'm not sure, but I've always believed the one given to me was taken off a dead Japanese soldier. Those brown spots look like blood to me."

"No, I mean, Leonard, did you carry our flag?"

He shook his head no. "I didn't carry any in my pocket, but some of the Japanese did." Then, perhaps wanting to change the subject, he pointed to one of the photos. "That's my grandson, Justin. He really got the works on our second trip in 2005. His hair was down to here." He indicated several inches below his collar. "He got it cut though."

"Like a Marine?" I asked.

"Yeah, he's a good boy too," he said proudly. "Good looking, good athlete, good student!"

"Did he join the Marines?"

"No, he's in school."

"There were three hundred twenty people on the second tour," Dick commented. "Eighty-seven were veterans! Quite a difference from the first trip, when there were only seven vets. Knowing a little more about what to expect made for a more enjoyable trip the second time."

"Sorry to interrupt your story," Dick's wife, Susan, said, as she strolled into the room.

"No problem," we assured her.

"So nice to meet you, after hearing so much about you," she remarked, embracing me with a hug and a kiss.

"Same to you, and this is another Susan, my daughter," I said, pointing towards her. She received the same cordial greeting.

"See my flower? Isn't it beautiful?" Leonard asked her.

"Very nice," she said, smiling at him. "How's Leonard doing? Are you asking him any questions? Go ahead, ask him, lots of them. Dick will talk all day if you let him."

"He's doing exceptionally well and has answered several questions. He's told us some stories on his own, also. Did he ever tell you about the young Marine in his twenties who suffered through a painful circumcision? Or about the toilet paper, or lack thereof, at Camp Tarawa? Or how unhappy he was when he didn't get to show off his prowess in baseball, because they had to prepare to leave for Iwo before he got a chance to bat? My favorite, however, was his tale of going AWOL before deploying to Iwo Jima. I'm so sorry he's had a stroke, he probably has a million tales to tell and now they are all locked up in his memory bank," I said wistfully. "The ones we've heard are all fun experiences and those are the ones to remember. I never tell my bad experiences, just the good. Let's hope Leonard's bad ones are nothing but shadows now."

Susan asked, "Have you done the flag?"

"Yes, and taken lots of pictures. Still need some of the four of us together. All of you have played such an important role in this story."

"You most of all," Dick remarked. "You kept the flag all these years."

"Thanks," I replied.

Arranging our chairs so Leonard and I were side by side, we held the flag in front of us, while my daughter and Dick stood in back of us with the beautiful stained glass wall hanging serving as the background.

Dick's wife called, "Everyone ready? Eins, zwei, drei, cheese!"

Huh! I never heard that before, I thought, but it worked. We all laughed.

"I'll trade places with you, Susan," my daughter said. "I kinda like that eins, zwei, drei stuff. Is everybody ready? Eins, zwei, drei, cheese!" she said laughingly, and we all smiled.

Peals of laughter rang out when someone remarked, "Must be some German heritage around here." Turned out we all did.

As I noticed my daughter taking pictures of Leonard and me just sitting there while I folded the flag, I stopped her.

"Mother, I don't want posed pictures. Just act natural."

"Okay, but I'm going to hold Leonard's hand." Looking up at him with an impish smile, I said, "Might call this flirting, but it's just for my friends at the VA. Some think there's more to this visit than I told them. They'll enjoy seeing this."

"You won't mind that at all, will you, Leonard?" my daughter joked.

"Oh, no," he replied, and grinned at me with that twinkle in his eyes.

"I'll bet you didn't know you'd be so photographed today, but mother likes pictures, they are her treasures and enrich her memories."

"No, I didn't, but she's sweet and I'm happy she came. You look like her."

"Yes, that's what I'm told. When we're together around my friends, they always say, 'That's what you have to look forward to.'"

Susan Wehry, Dick Rogers,
Maxine Wehry and Leonard Mooney

Chapter Twelve

I continued holding Leonard's hands as Dick told about taking Leonard to see the movie, Flags of Our Fathers.

"When I heard it was coming to Hackettstown, I told Susan we had to take Leonard. He was quite adamant about not going. 'I haven't been to a movie in forty-seven years and see no reason for starting now,' he told us. Eventually we persuaded him to go and promised we would leave if he was uncomfortable reliving the story. At times he would comment, 'that's not true,' or, 'that's not the way it happened.' When the movie ended and the lights were turned on, I stood up and asked for their attention.

"It isn't often we are privileged to have one of the men portrayed in the movie sitting in the audience. Tonight, the radioman in the movie is here. He is a hometown man, my uncle, Leonard Mooney."

"They all applauded, and came by to shake his hand."

"He made you a hero again, didn't he, buddy," I said, and gave him a reassuring pat on the hand. Like most servicemen, I knew, Leonard wanted no notoriety and felt no heroism for having done his part in bringing the surrender of Japan and peace to the Pacific. Their war stories stay hidden except at times when they 'shoot the bull' with other veterans, even the women. I've experienced this in my work at the VA Medical Center. Veterans understand veterans and my pat on Leonard's hand let him know I understood.

"What did you think of the movie, Leonard?" my daughter asked. "Was it fairly accurate, or was it too much fiction?"

"Glorified war movie!" he responded. "If his father was alive they wouldn't have made it. He would not have let them."

"Wonder why his son wanted it made?" she further asked.

"Don't know," was his response.

Speaking for myself, I can think of two reasons. I'm hoping it was because he was so proud of his father and those others, he wanted the whole world to know about them. I would have felt the same if it had been my father. I have read the book, and was very touched by what I learned about the men whose lives were immortalized and by the details of why Iwo Jima was so important for us to capture and become an American base.

My daughter continued asking Leonard questions. "Did you not talk about the war because you were sad, or just humbled by what you had experienced?"

"I was sad. I missed my buddies. I wanted to forget what happened to them. I wondered what kind of life they may have had, marriage, careers, children, grandchildren. I got to have it all."

"Did you enlist?"

"Yes."

"How long did you serve?"

"Four years. I was twenty-eight when I went in and thirty-two when discharged."

"Were you married?"

"No, single."

Dick broke in, "After the war, he married my aunt, Dad's sister. He had gone back in the banking business, and eventually retired from there. Life was good to him until my aunt's death. She had early signs of Alzheimer's, but her death came after a fall in their kitchen. When 911 responded, they discovered her hip was broken. She seemed to be progressing in rehab, but died on her way back to the hospital from major complications. That was in 2003. She was eighty-four."

"Six years younger than me," Leonard remarked.

Speaking about their family reminded me that I had brought photos of mine to share, and I proceeded to remove them from my purse. "This is my husband Al, Leonard. He wasn't a Marine, but a sergeant in the Army. His tour of duty was spent with the 80th Division, 317th Infantry, in the European War Theater. We met after the war in Vincennes, where I worked in E. R. Pulliam's Jewelry Store. He was a salesman for Klein Brothers Jewelry Company in Cincinnati, Ohio. He was a Kentucky boy from Newport across the Ohio River from Cincinnati. We were married for forty years, until his death, September 7, 1988, on the golf course."

"He's a nice looking man," Leonard said.

Naturally, I agreed with him, and exhibited two photos taken with my children. One had been taken at my son's in Pensacola, and the other at Christmas at my condo in 2009. I picked up the one at Pensacola. "This is my daughter Kay, it's her sixtieth birthday."

"Is she your eldest?" Dick asked.

"Yes, and then: Susan; Jeanne and her husband, Gerald; Mark and his wife, Laura, and their dog, Benji; and Joe, my youngest, who served in the Marine Corps Reserves for six years. I keep reminding him he'd be ready for retirement soon, had he stayed in, but then he reminds me he could be dead, too!"

Leonard picked up the Christmas picture. "I like this," he said. "Christmas is always a good time with family."

"So true, but I also like Thanksgiving. You can have fun and not worry about gifts to buy, and they are all around your table."

I then showed them pictures of my grandchildren and great grandchildren.

Chapter Thirteen

"Leonard, here's a picture of a dog named George. Apparently he was a mascot of your outfit. At least, that's what I had on the back of the original."

"I know we had a dog, but I don't remember anything about it."

"Wonder what kind he is?" I asked.

"A dog, dog," Dick said.

"Well, you can have George if you wish, I have another one at home."

"Thank you," he said, and stared at the picture as if trying to remember. Our driver, guide, chaperone, or whatever he was, may have been a Sgt. Larsen or Lafton. He may have been George's caretaker, as I had photos of them together. They were discarded with several photos when I thought I'd never hear from Leonard. I remember he had a health problem relating to his lungs, and he was very friendly and helpful."

"By the way, while rummaging through photo albums and scrapbooks, I found our schedule for that weekend. We certainly couldn't have gotten into any trouble, as our actual time with those Marines was limited. We left our base at 0730 on May 26, 1945, and went to the Naval Air Station. We flew from there at 0915 and arrived at Upolu Point, NAS, on the big island of Hawaii, at 1015. Our flight over was a little nerve-wracking, as the Marine mechanic on board kept checking the engines."

"What's wrong?" Lt. Virginia Ballard, our chaperone, asked.

"A small oil leak, no big deal," he replied.

"Maybe not to you, I thought, but I sure don't want to end up as a big splat on the ground or drowned in the ocean thousands of miles from home. Eventually, I became brave enough to peek out the window. 'Hey,' I yelled, 'did you know they had cows in Hawaii? Look out your windows.'

"Some were as amazed as me, because our barracks, in fact our base, was surrounded by cane fields. I had assumed the rest of the island was pineapple fields since, so we had been told,

Dole's pineapple plant was in Honolulu. We also had become accustomed to the radio announcer bellowing over the air waves each morning, "There will be, or there will not be, work in the pineapple fields today!"

"Cattle just didn't fit in the picture. Learned later that the big island of Hawaii is one of the largest beef producers in the US.

"After landing we were transported by trucks or bus to the WR Barracks in the Hospital Wing of Camp Tarawa and arrived there at 1130, chose our beds, stored our gear and continued to the Sgt.'s Mess for lunch. After lunch we returned to our barracks, rested and changed into appropriated clothing for the beach. From my picture, I realize Marian and I changed into our bathing suits, but I have no recollection of having done so.

"We arrived at Marine Beach at 1400 and spent time swimming, talking and taking pictures before our barbecue dinner was served from 1530 to 1700.

"Probably this is where I met Lonnie Crowell and the other Marine in the photos, because one of my discarded pictures was of them, lounging on the beach in their khakis.

"How we met and discovered we were both from Indiana remains a mystery. My only memory was discussing the rivalry between our high schools in sports as he was from Evansville only sixty miles or less south of Vincennes, my hometown.

"I'm sure these two young Marines and Hoosiers, thousands of miles from home, stayed together as much as possible that weekend. This time, it was a kindred spirit of home!

"No doubt we rode in separate vehicles from the beach back to our barracks in Camp Tarawa. This would certainly have discouraged any thoughts of excessive fraternization between the WRs and male Marines, some of whom may have looked across the crowded beach and saw a stranger they were sure was their one true love!

"Those adult chaperones sure knew how to make plans that worked, didn't they?

"Arriving back in camp we showered, rested and dressed in our uniforms for the dance. It was held at the USO, wherever that was, from 1845 to 2130.

"Bed check was 2200! That's 10 PM in case you can't figure military time. Can you imagine having a curfew like that for seventeen-to-twenty-year-olds today? I can't…even though it might be a good idea.

"I've never had a penchant for dancing, too self conscious, but apparently I enjoyed this evening. My notes tell me these Marines were great dancers!

"Sunday, May 27 arrangements were made for religious services, however, I don't remember attending any. We ate breakfast at the Sgt.'s Mess where a Marine by the name of "Ski" served me his eggs. Supposedly it was the only Mess Hall to have them. " (I'm borrowing one of Leonard's quotes - he must have thought I was alright!)

"Later we visited the Red Cross hut and the Convalescent Hospital #1 where we visited a great group of less severely injured war heroes. They were so appreciative of our visit and we had our pictures taken with them. Did any of us girls realize at the time what sacrifices our Marines had made on that small volcanic rock in the Pacific called Iwo Jima? I doubt it.

"Sometime between breakfast and lunch, may have been when Lonnie Crowell gave me the Japanese Flag. Our picture with the other Marine was taken with a Quonset hut in the background. This must have been somewhere in Camp Tarawa, where Leonard said they stayed until being deployed to Japan as part of our occupational forces.

"We ate lunch at the Sgt.'s Mess before retrieving our luggage and leaving for NAS Upolu Point at 1400 or 1500. On our way, we toured the Big Island and what is still a vivid remembrance was the steam escaping through the lava rock somewhere along the route. It frightened me!

On our flight home there was no one on board checking for an oil leak, so they either repaired our plane, or gave us a new one. I was probably too excited to be afraid of flying. We arrived safely home at MCAS #61, Ewa, Oahu at 1845. Tired but in good spirits."

Did we make a difference to those young Marines that weekend? I hope so. Perhaps, for a short time, we helped erase from their minds, the terrible experiences and sacrifices they had seen occur, just two months before our visit. If so, I'm happy to have been a part of it.

I now wonder, when did they realize how quickly they had matured into manhood from those eager young boys who had been so gung-ho to serve their country? It really doesn't matter, I'm just proud to call them brothers.

Dick brought me back to the present when he remarked, "You sure have taken good care of that flag."

"Thanks, but we might have found everyone alive whose names are on it, had I examined it more closely years ago. It lay for years in my memorabilia box until the day I decided to put it in the envelope for fear of it getting ruined by the pins and airmen's wings and my ID bracelet." I must have had a nostalgic moment the day I removed it from the envelope and discovered those three names.

"Never in my wildest dreams would I have ever thought the flag would become such a highlight in my life and bring me all the way to Hackettstown, New Jersey, where I would meet such wonderful friends and a handsome Marine whose name on the flag now has a face to go with it. I am so happy the good Lord let Leonard live so long!

"By the way, Dick, do you have my letter?"

"It's here someplace, but I'm keeping it"

Leonard chorused the same, and continued, "I'm getting a lawyer..." We were all laughing so heartily, the rest of his response was lost in the clamor.

"I don't care if I have it, but I would like a copy. I just want to know what I wrote."

"I'll mail you a copy. Would you like for me to read it to you? Here it is."

"Thanks, but first, is there a date on it?"

"Let's see. Yeah, it's April. April 23,2008"

I leaned over, tapped Leonard's knee, and with a mischievous grin, chided him, "Leonard, that was two years ago. Why did you wait so long to answer?"

Grinning, he squeezed my hand and replied, "Don't know."

We had so much fun sitting there listening and holding hands. As Dick began reading, it became laughable when we realized Dick had read the last page first.

I have to admit it wasn't the best letter I've ever written, but I'm happy I had the foresight to include my phone number and an address label at the conclusion. Using Marine Corps League note paper and enclosing the pictures, I had hoped would prove this was a legitimate inquiry and not a hoax.

Dick finally confessed, he was partially to blame for the delay in answering. Leonard had given it to him and it had gotten lost among other papers on his office desk.

"Well, I'm so thankful you had found it and it has had a happy ending," I told them.

Leonard asked Dick to tell about the Medal of Honor winner. It took a few minutes of dialogue between them before Dick realized to what he was referring.

"On our last trip to Iwo," Dick began, "this young Lady Marine approached Leonard and asked him if he knew a Medal of Honor winner by the name of Donald J. Ruhl."

"Oh, baby, do I know him. We went AWOL together. He went home to see his parents and I went to Sacramento."

"He got five hours of hard labor, splitting rocks," she said.

"All you got was fifteen minutes, Leonard?" I asked.

"Yeah, but…"

"Leonard's line of bull was better than his," Dick quipped.

"Is there anything else you can tell me about him?" she asked.

"Yes, he always wore a soft cap, a baseball cap, instead of his helmet."

"Anything else?"

"Yes, he always stood with his hands on his hips," Leonard told her.

She handed him a picture. "This is my father, Donald J. Ruhl. He's the reason I am wearing this uniform," she said.

Leonard had described him perfectly.

"She wanted to make sure you really knew him, didn't she?" my daughter asked.

"The story of his heroism and why he was awarded the Medal

of Honor is in Dick Wheeler's book, *IWO*," Dick remarked.

"Oh my gosh," I exclaimed, "that's a story in itself, I'll have to reread that part of the book. She must be so proud of him. No doubt she was touched deeply by finding one of her father's friends who knew all about his sacrifice. I wonder if she is making a career in the Marine Corps?

My daughter Susan informed us, "Susan has lunch prepared and we are to proceed to the dining room. First, Leonard, I'll have someone direct me to your room and I'll put the flower there. Is that okay by you?"

"Sure, thank you my dear."

Dick and I continued our conversation after they left, and gathered all the items he wanted me to have. Unplugging the camera, we joined them in a small private dining room.

As I entered the room, it looked so charming and hospitable. A round table with a red-checked tablecloth, china plates and silverware was near the center of the room with a lamp hanging above. To the side on separate tables was all the food: salad greens, fresh fruits, honey dew melon and cantaloupe, various cheeses, crackers, breads, meat and my favorite, poached and smoked salmon. The choice of drink was sodas, water, hot or iced tea and perhaps coffee, I'm not sure.

Susan commented she hadn't made the dessert, but had purchased blueberry cheesecake. It was an excellent choice and delicious. She was an excellent hostess and we complimented her, but 'thank you' didn't seem to be enough for all her preparations.

There was such a warm and friendly atmosphere as we ate and chatted about our families. We soon discovered our heritages were very similar: German, Irish and American Indian, but to mine I added English and French. As my father always said, "We were true-blooded Americans!"

Leonard began telling us about his wife's love for ceramics, then, described the china cupboard in the kitchen where she displayed her creations and collectibles.

Dick remarked she was a professional bowler on TV. They had built their home in 1954. Leonard began to smile, "My son Roger printed his name and 'Mom and Dad' in the wet cement."

"That will always be there," I remarked.

"Yes, that's why Leonard can't sell the house. Too many memories are there." Dick continued, "When Leonard's health problems first surfaced, we were told there was nothing further they could do except wait for him to die. We found another doctor who solved the major problem and we brought him here for rehab. That was last November or December. He's doing exceptionally well. We are all pleased and he's happy."

"It's certainly a friendly place," my daughter remarked.

"Yes, and efficient," Dick replied.

"Do you think he will ever return home?"

"We aren't for sure," Dick answered.

"Well, I hate to break up your party Leonard," Susan said, "but it's time to call it a day."

Reluctantly, I agreed, and a wave of nostalgia swept over me as I followed Leonard's wheelchair down the hall to the exit. My memorable visit which I had been anticipating for weeks was ending, but the fading name of Leonard J. Mooney on my souvenir Japanese flag was now represented by a kind, weathered, twinkly eyed, ninety-seven-year-old proud Marine's face.

My daughter and Dick continued photographing our departure.

I leaned over and placing both of my hands on either side of his face, I said, "Thank you, honey, for this wonderful day. It's been great. You will never know how much this has meant to me. I am so happy to have met you," and gave him a kiss.

"Thank you dear, me too."

"Neither of us could possibly have known we'd be celebrating this day sixty-five years after I had received the flag you had signed, but I hope you have enjoyed it as much as me. It's been awesome!"

I smiled at him as I turned to leave; he was smiling, but his eyes looked sad and not twinkling.

"Aloha," I said and walked away.

Dick and his wife Susan were standing near the door. My daughter and I embraced them both. We thanked Susan for her devotion to Leonard and for making our day special.

We rode with Dick back to his office to retrieve our car.

Conversation centered on Leonard and his ability to relate to our questions, join in our discussions and tell some of his own stories. This was quite a feat for a ninety-seven-year-old who had been stricken with one or more strokes. We thanked Dick for his interesting narratives, for being so attentive to Uncle Leonard and for revealing to us who the real Leonard Mooney, my hero, really was and is.

As I gave him a goodbye hug and kiss, I thanked him again for making our visit so memorable and exciting.

"See you on Leonard's 100th," I said.

"It's been the same for me," he replied. "Thanks for coming."

Susan opened the car doors and a blast of heat exited the car. It felt like 150° mixed with the outside temperature of over 100°. We waited awhile for the car to cool, then headed towards Burlington, Vermont, a few hundred miles away.

I can honestly say this trip was one of the most memorable of any I've taken. I now knew that the flag that had originated in Japan and traveled various ways to Iwo Jima, Hawaii, California, Indiana, Kentucky, Florida and Hackettstown, New Jersey would someday perhaps be in the Marine Corps Museum, Quantico, Virginia. What an historic, sad, exciting and interesting trip for all who were involved in its journey.

Susan and Dick Rogers
Maxine Wehry, and Leonard Mooney

Maxine Cardinal in Hawaii cane fields

Lt. Ballaard (background) and Lucy Newman (front)

A FLAG A LETTER A ROSE
May 26-27, 1945   July 7, 2010

Photo book of Maxine Wehry's and Leonard Mooney's visit.

Leonard J. Mooney and Maxine Wehry
"The end of our visit."

The Epilogue

It was a long drive back to Burlington, Vermont, and the adrenaline ran rampant. Our trip to Hackettstown, New Jersey had been so exhilarating and our chattering resembled a nest of magpies. We were two happy people hoping our new friends we had just left were experiencing the same type of happiness.

Arriving home we sent an email to inform them we had arrived safely and thanked them again for their hospitality and all they had done to make our visit so memorable.

The following day dawned almost as hot as the previous one had been. It was hard to fathom that Vermont could be hotter than Florida. "Listen to what I found among my emails," Susan shouted that evening from her office, which was adjacent to my bedroom. It's from Dick in answer to your email."

"'Howdy, yes, it worked out better than I thought. The weather is what we worried about the most. Susan was with Leonard for several hours today. She had him sign two copies of the book *IWO* for you. When we put the video footage on a disk from the pictures, I'll send the books and the disc to you. She said he couldn't stop telling her how happy he was seeing and meeting you. You made his dream come true. You rolled his life back sixty-five years. You're his angel now. Thank you.'"

"Well, it seems our visit was as enjoyable and meaningful to Leonard as it was to you, Mother," Susan remarked. We both smiled in acknowledgement.

The following week, Susan and I, with the help of our Apple computer, were able to design and order a hardback book with pictures and a story pertaining to our trip. We titled it, "A Flag - A Letter - A Rose" and it became the launch for my writing this book, "A Kindred Spirit."

Later, I sent Leonard a small framed picture of us with the flag. In the accompanying letter, I expressed the hope again that it would not conjure up old war memories but only the fun memories of two aging, young-at-heart Marines who had an unbelievable and enjoyable first meeting. Dick related to us that the picture is now on Leonard's bedside table and because of his "angel" he's sleeping better. That brought a smile to my face and a memory to cherish.

When the holidays came, I was surprised and yet elated to receive a card from Leonard. There on the front of it was Leonard and me with the flag! The enclosed Christmas letter sent to everyone explained my presence. I felt like a celebrity!

The Rogers and I continue our emails, and occasionally I'll drop a card or note to Leonard. My prayer is that we will both be healthy enough to meet again on his 100th birthday, April 6, 2013. Wouldn't that be awesome?

Pursuing my quest to find the identity of Lonnie Crowell in the picture, I enlisted the aid of the Marine Corps League Detachment #1007 in Vincennes, Indiana, of which I am a charter member. Herschel Hamm, a fellow member, became very interested in my story and contacted another Marine, Robert M. Reuter, adjutant of River City Detachment #1090 in Evansville, Indiana. Their interest and endeavors have been outstanding. Through them, I know a few important details about PFC Lonnie Crowell of Easy Company, 2/28, Fifth Marine Division. He was MOS 746 (automatic rifleman) BAR in WW2. Born in 1926, died April 19, 1979, at age 53 from a heart attack. He worked in maintenance for the Executive Inn in Evansville. His wife was Doris, two children, Charles and Susan Wigginton and a brother, George. Buried in Cave Springs Cemetery, Greenville, Kentucky.

I still have no absolute identification, but since he was a BAR Marine, and it was a heavy gun with ammunition, he needed to be muscular and strong. They have deduced the Marine on my right is Lonnie Crowell as he is the larger of the two. He is the same one Leonard and I had chosen. Perhaps someday we'll get our answer.

My story began because of a flag, but became an adventure of how four Marines' lives became intertwined by the action on Iwo Jima, a small volcanic island with black sand turned red by the blood of patriots from both countries. All lives were changed, but look what I discovered: there is a kindred spirit in the hearts of Marines which cannot be extinguished, even in death.

To all those men and women who have ever worn the Eagle, Globe and Anchor emblem: Semper Fi my friends and God bless!

Commandant James J. Jones with Members of the FL-2 Chapter of WMA at the 2002 Convention in Washington, DC
(L to R)
Eleanor Purser, Marie Halcomb, Commandant Jones, Lucille Gunion, Maxine Wehry and Marjorie Ellison

Joseph Wehry, USMCR   Maxine Cardinal Wehry

In Memorium

My dreams of visiting Leonard Mooney on his 100th birthday (April 4, 2013) were shattered when I received an E-mail from his nephew Dick Rogers stating Leonard had passed away peacefully on February 11, 2012. He now joins all those IWO buddies whom he never forgot. May they all rest in peace.

Leonard J. Mooney
April 4, 1913 - February 11, 2012

Lonnie Crowell
Died 1979

Gene Marshall
Died 1987

"SEMPER FI, MY HEROES"

Women Marines Association

About the Author

Maxine Cardinal Wehry, is the widow of Albert E. Wehry who died in 1988. She is the proud mother of five children Kay, Susan, Jeanne Rittinger, Mark and Joe; proud grandmother of Julie Kelly, Christina, Hillary, Sean and Devin; and proud great grandmother of Brooklyn and Dylan Kelly.

She retired after 23 years of Volunteer work in the Hospice Bereavement Unit at Bay Pines VA Hospital but continues to participate in their Memorial Services and in The Women Marines Association's FL-2 Chapter of which she has served as Vice President, Interim President, Historian, 'Nouncement writer, Sunshine Committee, and Assisted as Secretary & Chaplain.

She is a Life Member of The Women Marines Association, a Charter Member of WIMSA (Women In Military Service of America) and a Charter Member of The Marine Corps League Knox County Indiana Det. #1007.

She resides in Gulfport, FL and the flag is now in Hackettstown, NJ where it awaits its final destination.

Women in Military Service of America

Albert E. Wehry, Jr.

Maxine and Al Wehry
Wedding Day, June 19, 1948

(Back) Maxine, Kay, Joe and Laura
(Front) Gerald and Jeanne Rittinger, Susan, Mark and Benji

(Back) Julie Kelly, Maxine Wehry, Christina Wehry
(Middle) Sean, Hillary and (Front) Devin Wehry

Maxine Wehry with Dylan (L) and Brooklyn Kelly (R)

13831949R00050

Made in the USA
Charleston, SC
03 August 2012